Happy Birthday To Me!

by Barbara L. Luciano

PEARSON

Scott
Foresman

Editorial Offices: Glenview, Illinois • Parsippany, New Jersey • New York, New York
Sales Offices: Needham, Massachusetts • Duluth, Georgia • Glenview, Illinois
Coppell, Texas • Sacramento, California • Mesa, Arizona

Birthdays are special days!
In the United States we eat cake.

We sing "Happy Birthday."
We play games.

In Mexico children hit a piñata.
They get toys and candy.

In Russia children eat pie.
It is a birthday pie.

In Israel children sit in a chair.
Grownups lift the chair up!

How do you celebrate birthdays?

Glossary

birthday the day you were born

celebrate to have a special party